PEOPLES OF THE WORLD

Neil Morris

Introduction

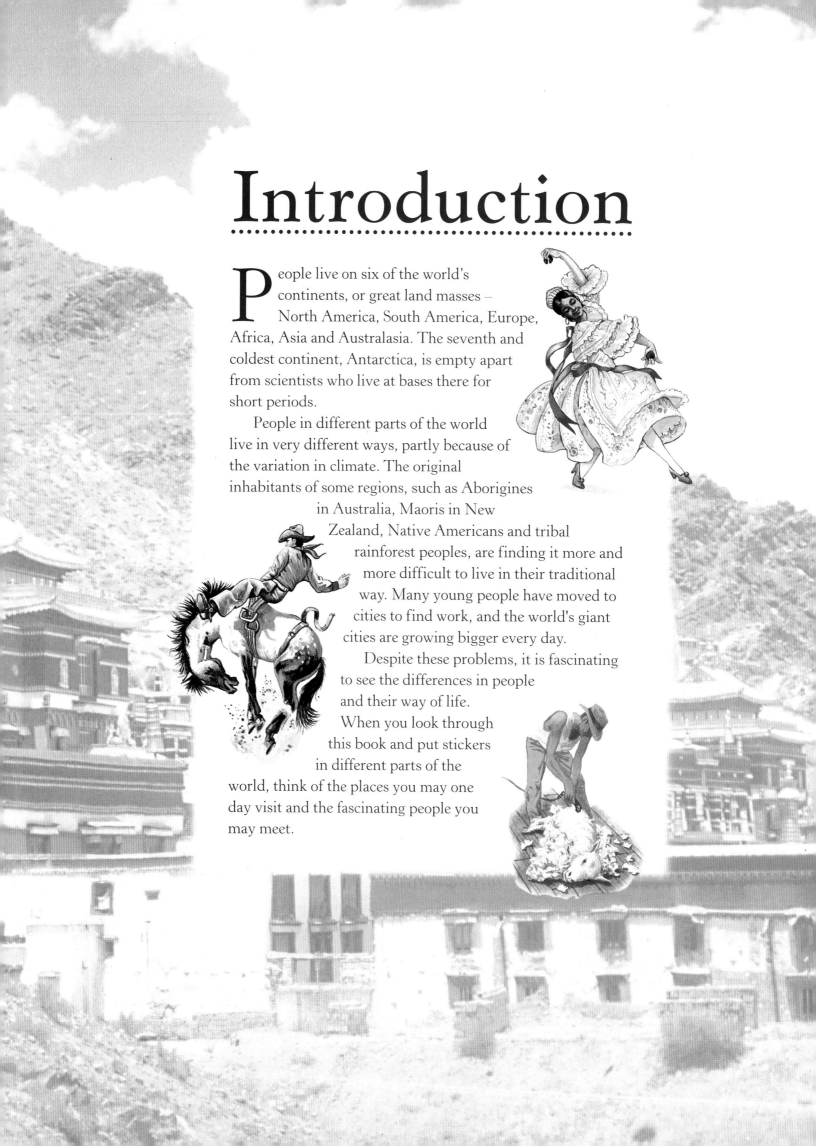

People live on six of the world's continents, or great land masses – North America, South America, Europe, Africa, Asia and Australasia. The seventh and coldest continent, Antarctica, is empty apart from scientists who live at bases there for short periods.

People in different parts of the world live in very different ways, partly because of the variation in climate. The original inhabitants of some regions, such as Aborigines in Australia, Maoris in New Zealand, Native Americans and tribal rainforest peoples, are finding it more and more difficult to live in their traditional way. Many young people have moved to cities to find work, and the world's giant cities are growing bigger every day.

Despite these problems, it is fascinating to see the differences in people and their way of life.

When you look through this book and put stickers in different parts of the world, think of the places you may one day visit and the fascinating people you may meet.

Fact file 1

Home run!

Baseball is often called "the great American pastime". In the USA and Canada, the top baseball competition is called the World Series, though no other countries take part! The game's rules were made in America, but they grew out of the European game of rounders. In baseball, the batter tries to hit the ball so that he can run around all the bases and score a run. If he manages to do this in one turn, he scores a "home run".

Did you know?

Ball games were played long before the modern versions, such as baseball, were invented. Many hundreds of years ago, Canadian Indians played a ball game called "baggataway". They used sticks with nets to carry the ball, and sometimes as many as a thousand warriors would play the game at one time! "Baggataway" developed into the modern sport of lacrosse.

Basketball

In 1891 James Naismith nailed two peach baskets at opposite ends of a balcony at his college in Massachusetts, USA. Then he gave two teams of students a soccer ball. The ball had to be thrown into a basket to score. The only problem was that someone then had to climb up to get the ball out again! This was the first game of basketball, and today the basket is a ring with an open net, so that the ball drops back down itself.

Did you know?

Ball games like basketball may date back 3000 years to a game played by a Native American people of Mexico. The Olmecs played a fast ball game on special courts built beside their temples. There were stone rings at either side of the court, and players scored points by hitting a solid rubber ball through a ring with their arms, elbows or hips – but not their hands.

The Americas

We call the original people of these continents Native Americans. They used to be called American Indians, because Christopher Columbus, after he had sailed across the Atlantic Ocean in 1492, thought he was in the East Indies. These original people range all the way from the frozen Arctic north, through hot plains and damp rainforests, to the cold southern tip of Chile.

RODEO
An American exhibition of cowboys' and cowgirls' skills.

AMERICAN FOOTBALLER
He wears a helmet and protective gear under his football uniform.

OAXACA WEAVER
The Mexican state of Oaxaca is famous for its woollen ponchos.

ICE-HOCKEY PLAYER
The national sport of Canada is fast, furious and very popular.

NEW ORLEANS JAZZ
Jazz musicians first played in New Orleans around 1900.

MARIACHI BAND
Mexican musicians sing and play guitars, trumpets and violins.

RIO CARNIVAL
A brilliant festival full of colourful costumes and street dancing.

NAVAJO
These Native Americans are farmers and herders around Arizona.

MEXICAN FIESTA
People enjoy holiday parades on these religious festivals.

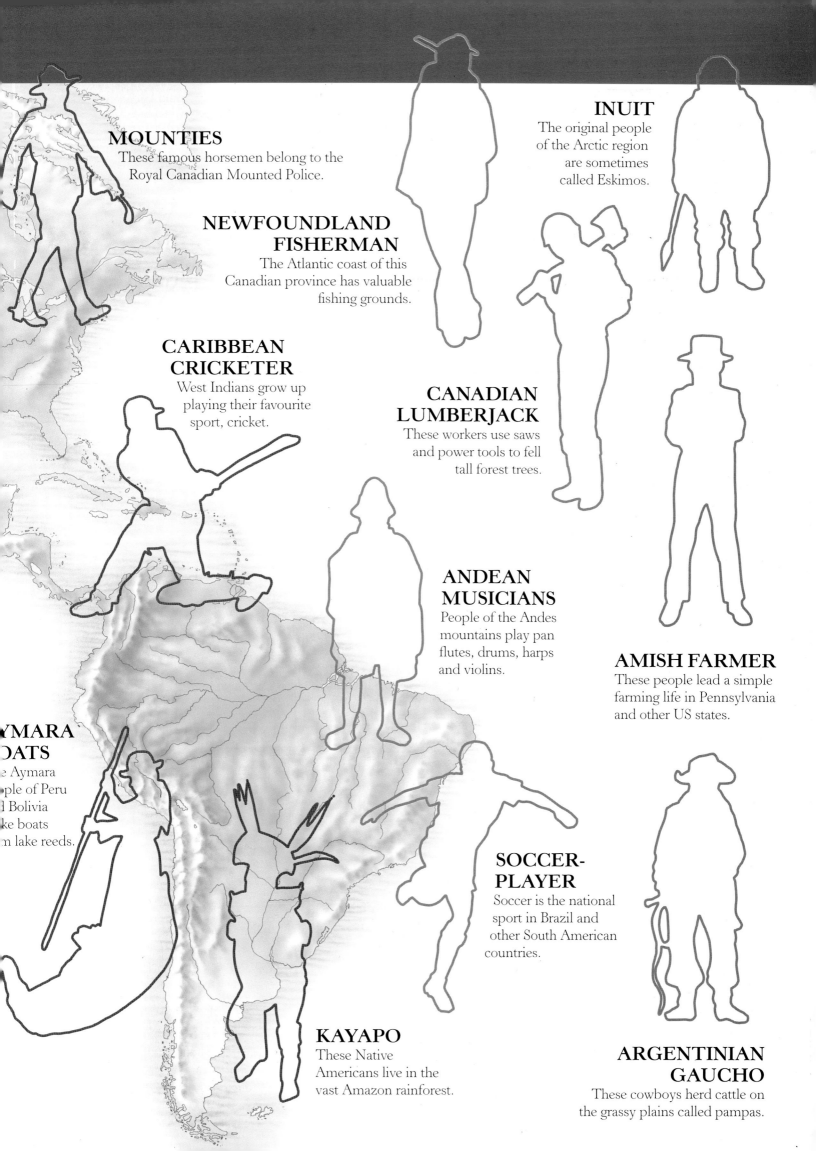

MOUNTIES

These famous horsemen belong to the Royal Canadian Mounted Police.

NEWFOUNDLAND FISHERMAN

The Atlantic coast of this Canadian province has valuable fishing grounds.

INUIT

The original people of the Arctic region are sometimes called Eskimos.

CARIBBEAN CRICKETER

West Indians grow up playing their favourite sport, cricket.

CANADIAN LUMBERJACK

These workers use saws and power tools to fell tall forest trees.

ANDEAN MUSICIANS

People of the Andes mountains play pan flutes, drums, harps and violins.

AMISH FARMER

These people lead a simple farming life in Pennsylvania and other US states.

YMARA OATS

e Aymara ple of Peru d Bolivia ke boats n lake reeds.

SOCCER-PLAYER

Soccer is the national sport in Brazil and other South American countries.

KAYAPO

These Native Americans live in the vast Amazon rainforest.

ARGENTINIAN GAUCHO

These cowboys herd cattle on the grassy plains called pampas.

Fact file 2

Mongolian yurt

On the plains and grasslands of Mongolia, wandering herdsmen and their families live in round tents called yurts. These are made of layers of felt covered with canvas or hide. A yurt is sturdy enough to stand up to strong winds, and is very warm in winter, with a hole in the top to let out smoke from the fire. The Mongols pack their yurts up and take them along when they move on with their herds of cattle and goats.

Did you know?

Many other people live in tents, but of a different kind. The Native Americans of the north-eastern woodlands covered the wooden frame of their tent homes with skin or bark. Plains Indians such as the Sioux also lived in tepees. The traditional tent of the Bedouin people, who wander the edges of the Arabian Desert, is made of goat or camel hair. This offers shelter from sandstorms and the heat of the desert.

A house carved into rock in the Cappadocia area, in Turkey.

Stilt houses

In many parts of the world, houses are built on stilts. The extra height off the ground or over water helps protect people from flooding caused by the rainy season or tropical storms. For this reason, people who live at the edge of Tonle Sap ("Great Lake"), in the south-east Asian country of Cambodia, build stilt houses of wood, bamboo or palm leaves. When the nearby Mekong River floods every October, their lake becomes four times bigger and much deeper.

Did you know?

The Aymara people live around the highest large lake in the world, Lake Titicaca. This lake lies on the border between Peru and Bolivia, high in the Andes mountains of South America. The Aymara live in houses similar to those of their ancestors, the Incas, and make boats from the local reeds. They use the reed boats to fish in the lake.

The Americas

Rio Carnival

American footballer

Mexican fiesta

Aymara boats

Mariachi band

Rodeo

Kayapo

Argentinian gaucho

Soccer-player

Inuit

The Americas

Ice-hockey player

Canadian lumberjack

Navajo

Newfoundland fisherman

Mounties

Oaxaca weaver

Amish farmer

Caribbean cricketer

Andean musicians

New Orleans jazz

Europe and Africa

Flamenco

Lapps

Gondolier

Alpine skier

Pelota

Bullfighting

Tour de France

Greek dancers

Palio

Polish costume

Europe and Africa

Zulu

Ndebele

Medicine man

Bororo

Yoruba

Pygmies

Masai

San

Moor

Tuareg

Asia and Australasia

Flying doctor

Maoris

Aborigines

Black pearls

Surfer

Sheep farmer

Spirit house

Canoeists

Australian Rules

All Blacks

Asia and Australasia

Sherpa

Mongol

Bedouin

Buddhist monk

Sumo wrestler

Marsh arab

Tea ceremony

Balinese procession

Karen

Balinese dancers

Vital statistics

Biggest cities
(population in millions)

1	Tokyo, Japan	25.0
2	New York, USA	19.7
3	São Paolo, Brazil	16.6
4	Mexico City, Mexico	15.1
5	Los Angeles, USA	15.0
6	Cairo, Egypt	14.5
7	Bombay, India	12.6
8	Buenos Aires, Argentina	12.5
9	Calcutta, India	11.1
10	Karachi, Pakistan	11.0

Did you know?
The population figures for the world's biggest cities refer to the large areas that include all the city's outer suburbs. Looking back to the year 1900, only two of today's biggest cities would have made the top ten: New York and Tokyo. Then the world's biggest city was London, with 6.4 million people, and the list included Paris, Berlin, Chicago, Vienna, St Petersburg, Philadelphia and Manchester.

Countries with the biggest population (in millions)

Did you know?
The most widely spoken language in the world is Mandarin Chinese. Mandarin is spoken by over 900 million people, but this is not the entire population of China. That's because there are many other Chinese dialects. Written Chinese has no alphabet, but is made up of about 50,000 characters. Each character forms a word or part of a word. Chinese children need to learn about 4000 characters in order to be able to read a book. The world's next most spoken language is English.

1	China	1213
2	India	936
3	USA	263
4	Indonesia	195
5	Brazil	156
6	Russia	147
7	Pakistan	141
8	Japan	125
9	Bangladesh	120
10	Nigeria	95

Europe and Africa

E urope is a small continent, and it is made up of many small countries, with their own peoples and traditions. Down the centuries, Europeans have travelled throughout the world, from Australia to Canada, to set up new societies. They also went to Africa, in search of land and slaves, and divided the continent into colonies. Today, most African peoples have regained their freedom and independence.

BULLFIGHTING
This spectacle can still be seen in Spanish rings, where matadors kill the bulls.

FLAMENCO
This style of guitar music and dance comes from southern Spain.

MOOR
Hundreds of years ago these people from north-west Africa ruled Spain.

PYGMIES
The Congo pygmies are thought to be the world's smallest people.

BORORO
Bororo youths from west Africa wear face masks to dance.

PELOTA
This is the favourite game of the Basque people of Spain and France.

SAN
The San people, or Bushmen, live around the Kalahari Desert of southern Africa.

YORUBA
These Nigerian people were once farmers, but many are now successful businessmen.

MASAI
These tall people keep cattle on the grasslands of Kenya and Tanzania.

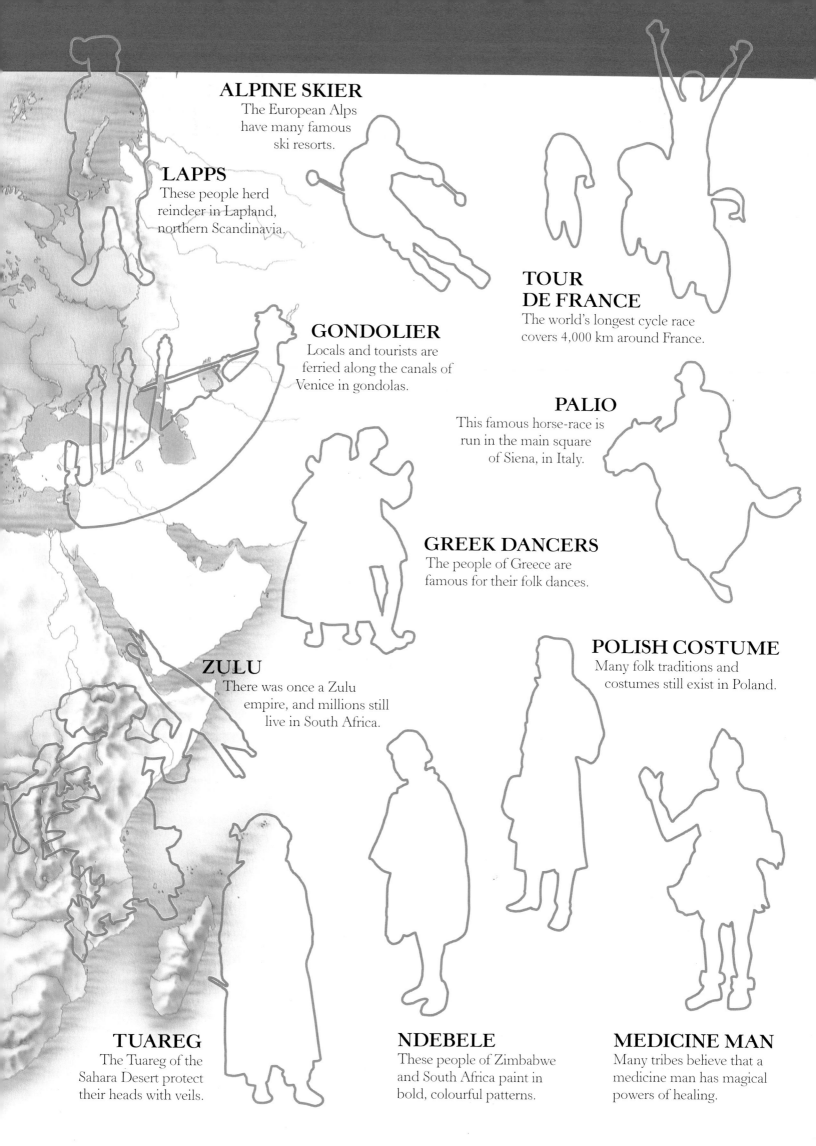

ALPINE SKIER
The European Alps
have many famous
ski resorts.

LAPPS
These people herd
reindeer in Lapland,
northern Scandinavia.

TOUR
DE FRANCE
The world's longest cycle race
covers 4,000 km around France.

GONDOLIER
Locals and tourists are
ferried along the canals of
Venice in gondolas.

PALIO
This famous horse-race is
run in the main square
of Siena, in Italy.

GREEK DANCERS
The people of Greece are
famous for their folk dances.

POLISH COSTUME
Many folk traditions and
costumes still exist in Poland.

ZULU
There was once a Zulu
empire, and millions still
live in South Africa.

TUAREG
The Tuareg of the
Sahara Desert protect
their heads with veils.

NDEBELE
These people of Zimbabwe
and South Africa paint in
bold, colourful patterns.

MEDICINE MAN
Many tribes believe that a
medicine man has magical
powers of healing.

Asia and Australasia

The world's first civilizations grew up in south-west Asia, in a region between the Tigris and Euphrates rivers. This is near where today's Marsh Arabs live. Asians travelled thousands of years ago to the continent of Australasia. European settlers arrived there only a little more than 200 years ago. Today, the Aborigines of Australia, as well as the Maoris of New Zealand, are gaining back some of their traditional lands from their governments.

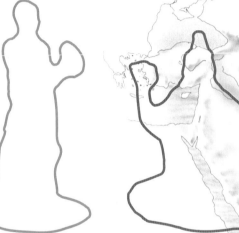

SHERPA
The mountain people of Nepal are farmers and traders, as well as mountaineers.

MARSH ARAB
These people live on the marshlands of Iraq, near the Tigris and Euphrates rivers.

BUDDHIST MONK
Buddhism was founded over 2500 years ago by an Indian prince.

BEDOUIN
These nomadic people wander the Arabian Desert with their camels and goats.

KAREN
The Karen people live in southern Myanmar, formerly known as Burma.

BALINESE DANCERS
The Indonesian island of Bali is famous for its wonderful dancers.

ABORIGINES
The original inhabitants of Australia travelled from Asia over 40,000 years ago.

SURFER
Surfing on the big rolling waves is a popular Australian sport.

BALINESE PROCESSION
The island of Bali has many famous parades and is popular with tourists.

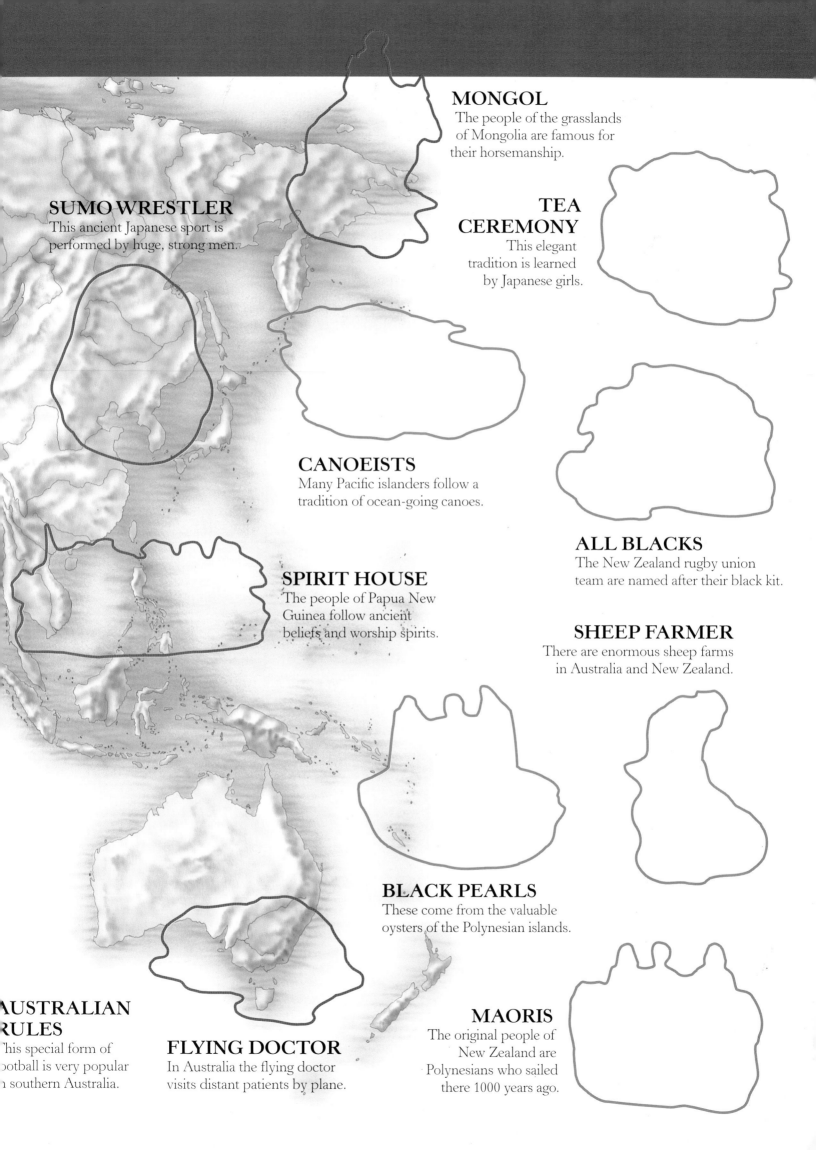

MONGOL
The people of the grasslands of Mongolia are famous for their horsemanship.

SUMO WRESTLER
This ancient Japanese sport is performed by huge, strong men.

TEA CEREMONY
This elegant tradition is learned by Japanese girls.

CANOEISTS
Many Pacific islanders follow a tradition of ocean-going canoes.

ALL BLACKS
The New Zealand rugby union team are named after their black kit.

SPIRIT HOUSE
The people of Papua New Guinea follow ancient beliefs and worship spirits.

SHEEP FARMER
There are enormous sheep farms in Australia and New Zealand.

BLACK PEARLS
These come from the valuable oysters of the Polynesian islands.

AUSTRALIAN RULES
This special form of football is very popular in southern Australia.

FLYING DOCTOR
In Australia the flying doctor visits distant patients by plane.

MAORIS
The original people of New Zealand are Polynesians who sailed there 1000 years ago.

Design: First Edition
Art Director: Clare Sleven
Project Manager: Susanne Bull
Production Assistant: Ian Paulyn
Artists: Clive Spong, Roger Stewart

This is a Parragon Book
This edition published in 2000
Parragon, Queen Street House, 4 Queen Street, Bath, BA1 1HE

2 4 6 8 10 9 7 5 3 1

Produced by Miles Kelly Publishing Ltd,
Bardfield Centre, Great Bardfield, Essex, CM7 4SL

British Library Cataloguing-in-Publication Data
A catalogue record for this book is available from the British Library

ISBN 0 75253 276 6

Printed in Italy
by STIGE Turin